THE
GRAND TOUR

PENHALIGON'S
SCENTED TREASURY
OF VERSE AND
PROSE

THE GRAND TOUR

EDITED BY SHEILA PICKLES

LONDON MCMXCI

For Penelope

CONTENTS

INTRODUCTION

Dear Traveller,

The Grand Tour originated in the eighteenth century when the children of wealthy families were sent to Europe to finish their education, to study the Arts and widen their horizons. The Romantic poets, Byron, Shelley, Keats and Browning then discovered the joys of the Mediterranean and wrote widely of Italy and Greece, which similarly attracted American writers and artists, such as Mark Twain and Henry James. The result was that in Victorian times a European Tour became as fashionable for Americans as for the British.

After the journey down to Dover, the Channel was crossed on the Calais Packet and, after an overnight stay, Paris was the first destination. The buildings seemed exquisite, the salons amusing, the manners delicate in an era when deportment was everything. Here the hungry travellers satisfied their palates with the best cuisine and quenched their thirsts with the finest wines. Then they travelled to Switzerland to the Alps and Lakes, where they enjoyed the masterpieces of nature. Thereafter Vienna provided the social pleasures of the opera and coffee houses, while further north the famous spas of Baden-Baden assisted recovery from over-indulgence. While the grand Gothic monuments of Germany proved inspiring, travellers were drawn further south by the promise of the sun. Through the mountain passes

and the gateway of Savoy into Italy – the land of Bel Canto – they anticipated an education both of the flesh and the spirit. Dr Johnson said, "A man who has not been in Italy is always conscious of an inferiority", and the travellers were to flock via the romantic lakes to the capitals of the diverse kingdoms yet to be united by Garibaldi. From Venice – one of the most romantic of cities, floating on the marshes where time had stood still for centuries – through Padua and Verona to Florence, a city inhabited by artists and craftsmen, the birthplace of Dante. And on to Siena for the Palio, the great horse-race; the Medieval Campo filled with the colourful pageantry of the contradas. Then a day each in Perugia and Assisi before setting off to the Holy City of Rome. Mindful of the scenes the City had witnessed in the Colosseum, the Forum and on the Seven Hills, and the mighty power of the Roman Catholic Church, most travellers spent time here before journeying south to Naples and perhaps on to Greece and the wonders of the Golden Age.

Travelling at that time was a leisurely affair, inspiration for the route coming from William Beckford's journey, as recounted in his *Dreams, Waking Thoughts, and Incidents*, and the details provided by Murray's Guides and Baedeker. Conditions were often uncomfortable and sometimes dangerous, but this did not deter writers, poets and spirited Victorian ladies in their quest for the old European classical world.

Thousands were to do the Tour and many were to write of it in their journals and diaries. The mode of transport, their adventures *en route* and their impressions of the art and architecture they were to find. The tales are so numerous and the opinions so varied that it has been hard to make a selection which both informs and entertains. I hope my final choice will inspire others on their travels.

I have chosen Penhaligon's Eau de Cologne to scent the endpapers of this Companion. Lord Byron, travelling with five servants, would certainly have taken such a Cologne with him, bottled in silver topped bottles in a rosewood *nécessaire* – an essential companion for a serious traveller, containing everything that was required for grooming and writing.

Sheila Pickles, Tuscany, 1990

THE Emperor Charles V used to say, that in proportion to the number of languages a man knew, he was so many more times a man. No one should think of travelling before he has made some acquaintance with the language of the country he is about to visit. This should be the first, as it is the best, preparation for a journey. It will prove as good as a double purse to him – as two pair of eyes, and one pair of ears – for, without it, the one pair he possesses is likely to be of little use.

JOHN MURRAY, 1745-1793

LA BELLE FRANCE

⌘❦⌘

" I never saw anything more beautiful
and gay than Paris "

QUEEN VICTORIA, 1819-1901

A VOYAGE AT SEA

DEAR HENRY, – A voyage at sea is like the voyage of life. How little we know at the beginning what we may see before the end! That Saturday morning when we left you standing on the pier at New York, we little thought what a week might bring. All was fair and promising. It was winter, and the Hudson was filled with floating ice; but the morning was clear, and the shores and the shipping all glittered in the sunlight. One could not witness a more beautiful spectacle than that as we passed down the bay. Once at sea, I felt the reaction which comes from long excitement, and only desired repose. The sea was not rough; and the Pereire, from her great length, balanced herself on the waves, rather than had that pitching motion which produces sea-sickness. Your thoughtfulness had secured me a whole state-room to myself, looking to the south; and there, with port-hole wide open, I inhaled the fresh air from the sea.

Tuesday was a delicious day. The air was mild as spring; the sun shone in a sky of azure; and our beautiful ship glided over a sea smooth as a mirror. We were going with all sails set, making seventeen knots an hour. The captain promised us, if this weather continued, we should be at Brest on Sunday evening. All the passengers were on the deck; and I made there, for the first time, the acquaintance of my *compagnons de voyage*. We remained on deck till night: it was so soft and spring-like, we could not resist the balmy air. It was a dispensation of Providence to prepare us for the trial which was to follow.

Wednesday, the barometer began to fall; and soon it became so rough, that it was impossible to leave my room. To add to the discomfort, every port-hole in the ship was closed, lest the sea should rush in; so that the air became close and stifling. The captain prepared himself well for the rising gale: and he had reason; for it grew worse and worse till Thursday evening, when it burst upon us with a violence that was terrific. That was a fearful night.

FROM *HOMES SKETCHES IN FRANCE* BY MRS HENRY FIELD

THE NOVELTY OF FRANCE

THE strait that separates England, so fortunately for her,
from the rest of the world, must be crossed many times
before a traveller ceases to be surprised at the sudden and
universal change that surrounds him on landing at Calais.
The scene, the people, the language, every object is new; and
in those circumstances in which there is most resemblance,
a discriminating eye finds little difficulty in discovering
marks of distinctions.

The noble improvement of a salt marsh, worked by Monsieur Mouron of this town, occasioned my acquaintance some time ago with that gentleman ; and I had found him too well informed, upon various important objects, not to renew it with pleasure. I spent an agreeable and instructive evening at his house. – 165 miles.

17th. Nine hours rolling at anchor had so fatigued my mare that I thought it necessary for her to rest one day ; but this morning I left Calais. For a few miles the country resembles parts of Norfolk and Suffolk ; gentle hills, with some enclosures around the houses in the vales, and a distant range of wood. The country is the same to Boulogne. Towards that town, I was pleased to find many seats belonging to people who reside there. How often are false ideas conceived from reading and report ! I imagined that nobody but farmers and labourers in France lived in the country ; and the first ride I take in that kingdom shows me a score of country seats. The road excellent.

Boulogne is not an ugly town ; and from the ramparts of the upper part the view is beautiful, though low water in the river would not let me see it to advantage. It is well known that this place has long been the resort of great numbers of persons from England, whose misfortunes in trade, or extravagance in life, have made a residence abroad more agreeable than at home. It is easy to suppose that they here find a *level* of society that tempts them to herd in the same place. Certainly it is not cheapness, for it is rather dear. The mixture of French and English women makes an odd appearance in the streets ; the latter are dressed in their own fashion ; but the French heads are all without hats, with close caps, and the body covered with a long cloak that reaches to the feet. The town has the appearance of being flourishing : the buildings good, and in repair, with some modern ones ; perhaps as sure a test of prosperity as any other. They are raising also a new church, on a large and expensive scale. The place on the whole is cheerful and the environs pleasing ; and the sea-shore is a flat strand of firm sand as far as the tide reaches.

FROM *TRAVELS IN FRANCE* BY ARTHUR YOUNG, 1741-1821

SPRING IN PARIS

I T was the day after their arrival in Paris, and the spring sunshine held Archer in his open window, above the wide silvery prospect of the Place Vendôme. One of the things he had stipulated – almost the only one – when he had agreed to come abroad with Dallas, was that, in Paris, he shouldn't be made to go to one of the newfangled "palaces".

"Oh, all right – of course," Dallas goodnaturedly agreed. "I'll take you to some jolly old-fashioned place – the Bristol say –" leaving his father speechless at hearing that the century-long home of kings and emperors was now spoken of as an old-fashioned inn, where one went for its quaint inconveniences and lingering local colour.

Archer had pictured often enough, in the first impatient years, the scene of his return to Paris . . . Sitting alone at night in his library, after the household had gone to bed, he had evoked the radiant outbreak of spring down the avenues of horse-chestnuts, the flowers and statues in the public gardens, the whiff of lilacs from the flower-carts, the majestic roll of the river under the great bridges, and the life of art and study and pleasure that filled each mighty artery to bursting. Now the spectacle was before him in its glory, and as he looked out on it he felt shy, old-fashioned, inadequate : a mere grey speck of a man compared with the ruthless magnificent fellow he had dreamed of being . . .

FROM *THE AGE OF INNOCENCE* BY EDITH WHARTON, 1862-1937

THE BOIS DE BOULOGNE

So here we are in the Avenue du Bois de Boulogne, at the head of the famous promenade, Jacob's Ladder, as it were, with angels ascending and descending going to the Bois or returning from the Bois – angels with yellow wigs, angels with raven black switches, angels who wear their hair in flat *bandeaux*, like the virgins in Perugino's pictures, angels whose heads suggest those of the dancing maidens of Tangara or the "majas" that Goya loved to paint. With huge hats or minute toques, mere garlands of sweet flowers, with garments that seem like a foam of lace and frills emerging from beneath long mantles of silk, velvet and brocade, the angels lean back voluptuously in elegant carriages, and graciously accord to mortals the calm spectacle of their various beauty and of their perfect toilets. From the Avenue du Bois de Boulogne the throng of carriages leads us to the Avenue des Acacias, the drive which fashion has selected in preference to more sunny, open, and picturesque avenues. And there between the gnarled and fantastic trunks of the acacia-trees the carriages advance slowly and with difficulty up and down, dazzling the eye with the radiant beauty of the blondes and brunettes, of angels ascending and descending, the joy of men.

Mingled with the carriages of the angels are the carriages of mortals, the landaus of the noble faubourg, the victorias of the club-men and ambassadors, the parade vehicles of all those who are afflicted with momentary or stable wealth. On foot, too, may be seen the young bloods, the pseudo-worldlings, the *pannés*, their eye-glasses fixed, correct and stiff, lounging with weary air, cackling and uttering flute-like squeaks of admiration as they watch the horses and the women, and waft salutations that are never returned. The afternoon drive in the Bois brings together, to see and to be seen, all the notabilities of fashionable Paris, the celebrities of society and of the stage, of leisure, of talent, of glory and of scandal.

FROM *IN PRAISE OF PARIS* BY THEODORE CHILD

THE QUEEN IN PARIS

St Cloud, 23rd August, 1855

I DO NOT intend to attempt any description, for I have no time for anything of the sort; besides I have no doubt you will read the papers, and I know good Van de Weyer has written *au long* to you about it all. I will therefore only give in a few words my impressions.

I am *delighted, enchanted, amused,* and *interested,* and think I never saw anything more *beautiful* and *gay* than Paris – or more splendid than all the Palaces. Our reception is *most* gratifying – for it is enthusiastic and really kind in the highest degree; and Maréchal Magnan (whom you know well) says that such a reception as I have received *every day here* is much greater and much more enthusiastic even than Napoleon on his return from his victories had received! Our entrance into Paris ... was quite *overpowering* – splendidly decorated – illuminated – immensely crowded – and 60,000 troops out – from the Gare de Strasbourg to St Cloud, of which 20,000 Gardes Nationales, who had come great distances to see me.

The Emperor has done wonders for Paris, and for the Bois de Boulogne. Everything is beautifully *monté* at Court – *very* quiet, and in excellent order; I must say we are both much struck with the difference between this and the poor King's time, when the noise, confusion, and bustle were great. We have been to the Exposition, to Versailles – which is most splendid and magnificent – to the Grand Opéra, where the reception and the way in which "God save the Queen" was sung were *most magnificent.* Yesterday we went to the Tuileries; in the evening *Théâtre ici*; to-night an immense ball at the Hôtel de Ville. They have asked to call a new street, which we opened, *after me!*

FROM *LETTERS OF QUEEN VICTORIA, 1819-1901*

BOHEMIAN LIFE

Rue de Lubeck, Paris, 1893. Coming home early this morning after a very noisy party in the Latin Quarter, I found your delightful letter. I have been drinking absinthe with poets and their loves. Bobbinette – isn't that a lovely name? – is a lovely creature, as delicate and innocent-looking and playful as if no such thing as the marriage-bond existed, and as if Latin Quarter manners set the code of morals for the world. I have been having a most amusing time with these queer people – all so gracious and friendly to me. I never really touched the life of Paris before.

To-day I have a breakfast-party at St Germain. My guests will be arriving – poets in straw hats and pink shirts.

FROM *THE LIFE AND LETTERS OF SIR EDMUND GOSSE*, 1849-1928

LUNCH AT LAURENTS

THE fresh spring sunshine which had so often attended Lizzie West on her dusty climb up the hill of St Cloud, beamed on her, some two years later in a scene and a situation of altered import.

Its rays, filtered through the horse chestnuts of the Champs Elysées, shone on the graveled circle about Laurent's restaurant; and Miss West, seated at a table within that privileged space, presented to the light a hat much better able to sustain its scrutiny than those which had shaded the brow of Juliet Deering's instructions.

Her dress was in keeping with the hat, and both belonged to a situation rife with such possibilities as the act of a leisurely luncheon at Laurent's in the opening week of the Salon. Her companions, of both sexes, confirmed this impression by an appropriateness of attire and an ease of manner implying the largest range of selection between the forms of Parisian idleness; and even Andora Macy, seated opposite, as in the place of co-hostess or companion, reflected, in coy greys and mauves, the festal note of the occasion.

FROM *THE LETTERS* BY EDITH WHARTON, 1862-1937

TOURAINE

NORMANDY is Normandy, Burgundy is Burgundy, Provence is Provence; but Touraine is essentially France. It is the land of Rabelais, of Descartes, of Balzac, of good books and good company, as well as good dinners and good houses. Georges Sand has somewhere a charming passage about the mildness, the convenient quality, of the physical conditions of central France – "*son climat souple et chaud, ses pluies abondantes et courtes.*" In the autumn of 1882 the rains perhaps were less short than abundant; but when the days were fine it was impossible that anything in the way of weather could be more charming. The vineyards and orchards looked rich in the fresh, gay light; cultivation was everywhere, but everywhere it seemed to be easy. There was no visible poverty; thrift and success presented themselves as matters of good taste. The white caps of the women glittered in the sunshine, and their well-made sabots clicked cheerfully on the hard, clean roads. Touraine is a land of old châteaux, – a gallery of architectural specimens and of large hereditary properties. The peasantry have less of the luxury of ownership than in most other parts of France; though they have enough of it to give them quite their share of that shrewdly conservative look which, in the little chaffering *place* of the market-town, the stranger observes so often in the wrinkled brown masks that surmount the agricultural blouse. This is, moreover, the heart of the old French monarchy; and as that monarchy was splendid and pictures-que, a reflection of the splendour still glitters in the current of the Loire.

FROM *A LITTLE TOUR IN FRANCE* BY HENRY JAMES, 1843-1916

MARKET MORNING

Iᴛ is market morning. The market is held in the little square outside, in front of the cathedral. It is crowded with men and women, in blue, in red, in green, in white; with canvassed stalls; and fluttering merchandise. The country-people are grouped about, with their clean baskets before them. Here, the lace-sellers; there, the butter and egg sellers; there, the fruit-sellers; there, the shoemakers. The whole place looks as it it were the stage of some great theatre, and the curtain had just run up, for a picturesque ballet. And there is the cathedral to boot: scene-like: all grim, and swarthy, and mouldering, and cold: just splashing the pavement in one place with faint purple drops, as the morning sun, entering by a little window on the eastern side, struggles through some stained-glass panes on the western.

In five minutes we have passed the iron cross, with a little ragged kneeling-place of turf before it, in the outskirts of the town; and are again upon the road.

FROM *GOING TROUGH FRANCE AND ITALY* BY CHARLES DICKENS, 1812-1870

A VILLA ON THE RIVIERA

IT was at this villa in Cannes that the Rostoffs passed the winter – and it wasn't at all the thing to remind Princess Rostoff that this Riviera villa, from the marble fountain – after Bernini – to the gold cordial glasses – after dinner – was paid for with American gold.

The Russians, of course, were gay people on the Continent in the gala days before the war. Of the three races that used Southern France for a pleasure ground they were easily the most adept at the grand manner. The English were too practical, and the Americans, though they spent freely, had no tradition of romantic conduct. But the Russians – there was a people as gallant as the Latins, and rich besides! When the Rostoffs arrived at Cannes late in January the restaurateurs telegraphed north for the Prince's favorite labels to paste on their champagne, and the jewelers put incredibly gorgeous articles aside to show to him – but not to the princess – and the Russian Church was swept and garnished for the season that the Prince might beg orthodox forgiveness for his sins. Even the Mediterranean turned obligingly to a deep wine color in the spring evenings, and fishing boats with robin-breasted sails loitered exquisitely offshore.

In a vague way young Val realized that this was all for the benefit of him and his family. It was a privileged paradise, this white little city on the water, in which he was free to do what he liked because he was rich and young and the blood of Peter the Great ran indigo in his veins. He was only seventeen in 1914, when this history begins, but he had already fought a duel with a young man four years his senior, and he had a small hairless scar to show for it on top of his handsome head.

But the question of love in the night was the thing nearest his heart. It was a vague pleasant dream he had, something that was going to happen to him some day that would be unique and incomparable. He could have told no more about it than that there was a lovely unknown girl concerned in it, and that it ought to take place beneath the Riviera moon.

FROM *LOVE IN THE NIGHT* BY F. SCOTT FITZGERALD, 1896-1940

ESSENTIAL LAUNDRY

I LEFT England in the autumn of 1862, intending to try whether the south of France was really, as I had been told, a cheaper place of abode than England. I travelled (for a lady) in rather a peculiar fashion, for I took with me only one small waterproof stuff bag, which I could carry in my hand, containing a spare dress, a thin shawl, two changes of every kind of under clothing, two pairs of shoes, pens, pencils, paper, the inevitable "Murray", and a prayer-book, so that I had no trouble or expense about luggage. My plan was to locate myself by the week, in any town or village that took my fancy, and ramble about on foot to botanize, and see all that was worth seeing in the environs ; and as I was "a lone woman", I took for my companion a mischievous but faithful and affectionate rough Scotch terrier, to be my guard and companion in my long solitary walks . . . There are disadvantages, however, in this gypsy style of travelling which I did not foresee when I set out.

It is impossible to get one's linen home from the laundress before the week's end, and sometimes they keep it eight or even ten days ; though, as a rule, the linen sent on Monday is brought back the following Saturday. They wash everything *au ruisseau*, in the cold water of the brook, using wood ashes instead of soap. The articles are all put to soak on the Monday night in a strong ley, previous to their being taken the next day to the stream ; and if you send clothes in the middle of the week, *they will be kept for the following week's wash.* In many places they are neither starched nor ironed, but simply sent home rough dry, though an Englishwoman will be charged the same prices as if they were properly got up, until she has learnt the real prices of the country. Everywhere, and in everything, an English person must expect to be charged twice as much as a Frenchwoman. The French ladies usually have their clothes washed by a *blanchisseuse*, and starched and ironed at home by a *repasseuse* or ironer, who goes out by the day. If, therefore, the traveller have but three of each article, *she must wash them herself and wear them rough dry.*

FROM *A LADY'S WALKS IN THE SOUTH OF FRANCE* BY MARY EYRE

MARSEILLES

WE left this town towards evening, and took the road to
Marseilles. . . . I was there twice or thrice afterwards,
in fair weather and foul; and I am afraid there is no doubt
that it is a dirty and disagreeable place. But the prospect,
from the fortified heights, of the beautiful Mediterranean,
with its lovely rocks and islands, is most delightful. These
heights are a desirable retreat, for less picturesque reasons –
as an escape from a compound of vile smells perpetually
arising from a great harbour full of stagnant water, and
befouled by the refuse of innumerable ships with all sorts of
cargoes: which, in hot weather, is dreadful in the last degree.

There were foreign sailors, of all nations, in the streets;
with red shirts, blue shirts, buff shirts, tawny shirts, and
shirts of orange colour. . . . There were the townspeople sitting
in clusters on the pavement, or airing themselves on the tops
of their houses, or walking up and down the closest and least
airy of Boulevards; and there were crowds of fierce-looking
people of the lower sort, blocking up the way, constantly.

FROM *GOING THROUGH FRANCE* BY CHARLES DICKENS, 1812-1870

A MEDITERRANEAN
PROMONTORY

To look at it from the outside, the Cap d'Antibes is just a long low spit of dull olive-grey land, but, within, it has sea and mountain views most gloriously beautiful. To the east you see everything you can see from Nice, to the west you see everything you can see from Cannes; to the north, a gigantic range of snow-covered Alps; to the south, and all around, the sky-blue Mediterranean. For the Cape is a promontory made up of lots of little promontories, each jutting into the sea at all possible angles, and with endless miniature bays, mimic islets, their white rocks jagged and worn by the dashing waves, that break over them in ceaseless spray, even in glassy weather. To sit among oranges, olives, and palms, as at Algiers or Palermo, and yet look up from one's seat under one's vine and fig-tree, to see the snow-clad Alps glowing pink in the sunset as at Zermatt or Chamonix, is a combination of incongruous delights nowhere else to be met in Europe.

FROM *THE RIVIERAS* BY AUGUSTUS HARE, 1792-1834

WANDERLUST

"Hills peep o'er hills, and Alps on Alps arise!"

ALEXANDER POPE, 1688-1744

THE STIMULATION OF
THE ALPS

To any one who should come from a southern sanatorium to the Alps, the row of sun-burned faces round the table would present the first surprise. He would begin by looking for the invalids, and he would lose his pains, for not one out of five of even the bad cases bears the mark of sickness on his face. The plump sunshine from above and its strong reverberation from below colour the skin like an Indian climate ; the treatment, which consists mainly of the open air, exposes even the sickliest to tan, and a tableful of invalids comes, in a month or two, to resemble a tableful of hunters. But although he may be thus surprised at the first glance, his astonishment will grow greater, as he experiences the effects of the climate on himself. In many ways it is a trying business to reside upon the Alps : the stomach is exercised, the appetite often languishes ; the liver may at times rebel ; and because you have come so far from metropolitan advantages, it does not follow that you shall recover. But one thing is undeniable – that in the rare air, clear, cold, and blinding light of Alpine winters, a man takes a certain troubled delight in his existence which can nowhere else be paralleled. He is perhaps no happier, but he is stingingly alive. It does not, perhaps, come out of him in work or exercise, yet he feels an enthusiasm of the blood unknown in more temperate climates. It may not be health, but it is fun.

FROM *ESSAYS OF TRAVEL* BY ROBERT LOUIS STEVENSON, 1850-1894

AN OUTING TO CHILLON

W INTERBOURNE'S eyes followed them; he was indeed
quite mystified. He lingered beside the lake a quarter
of an hour, baffled by the question of the girl's sudden
familiarities and caprices. But the only very definite
conclusion he came to was that he should enjoy deucedly
"going off" with her somewhere.

Two days later he went off with her to the Castle of
Chillon. He waited for her in the large hall of the hotel, where
the couriers, the servants, the foreign tourists were lounging
about and staring. It wasn't the place he would have chosen

for a tryst, but she had placidly appointed it. She came tripping downstairs, buttoning her long gloves, squeezing her folded parasol against her pretty figure, dressed exactly in the way that consorted best, to his fancy, with their adventure. He was a man of imagination and, as our ancestors used to say, of sensibility; as he took in her charming air and caught from the great staircase her impatient confiding step the note of some small sweet strain of romance, not intense but clear and sweet, seemed to sound for their start. He could have believed he was *really* going "off" with her. He led her out through all the idle people assembled – they all looked at her straight and hard : she had begun to chatter as soon as she joined him. His preference had been that they should be conveyed to Chillon in a carriage, but she expressed a lively wish to go in the little steamer – there would be such a lovely breeze upon the water and they should see such lots of people. The sail wasn't long, but Winterbourne's companion found time for many characteristic remarks and other demonstrations, not a few of which were, from the extremity of their candour, slightly disconcerting. To the young man himself their small excursion showed so far delightfully irregular and incongruously intimate that, even allowing for her habitual sense of freedom, he had some expectation of seeing her appear to find in it the same savour. But it must be confessed that he was in this particular rather disappointed. Miss Miller was highly animated, she was in the brightest spirits ; but she was clearly not at all in a nervous flutter – as she should have been to match *his* tension ; she avoided neither his eyes nor those of any one else ; she neither coloured from an awkward consciousness when she looked at him nor when she saw that people were looking at herself.

FROM *DAISY MILLER* BY HENRY JAMES, 1843-1916

ALPINE FLOWERS

W E found, indeed, more interest in the wild-flowers than in anything else. We gathered a specimen or two of every kind which we were unacquainted with; so we had sumptuous bouquets. But one of the chief interests lay in chasing the seasons of the year up the mountain and determining them by the presence of flowers and berries which we were acquainted with. For instance, it was the end of August at the level of the sea; in the Kandersteg valley, at the base of the Pass, we found flowers which would not be due at the sea level for two or three weeks; higher up we entered October, and gathered fringed gentians. I made no notes, and have forgotten the details, but the construction of the floral calendar was very entertaining while it lasted.

In the high regions we found rich store of the splendid red flower called the Alpine rose, but we did not find any example of the ugly Swiss favourite called *Edelweiss*. Its name seems to indicate that it is a noble flower and that it is white. It may be noble enough, but it is not attractive, and it is not white. The fuzzy blossom is the colour of bad cigar ashes, and appears to be made of a cheap quality of grey plush. It has a noble and distant way of confining itself to the high altitudes, but that is probably on account of its looks; it apparently has no monopoly of those upper altitudes, however, for they are sometimes intruded upon by some of the loveliest of the valley families of wild-flowers. Everybody in the Alps wears a sprig of Edelweiss in his hat. It is the native's pet, and also the tourist's.

FROM *A TRAMP ABROAD* BY MARK TWAIN, 1835-1910

THE ESSENTIAL COMPANION

A FLASK, to hold brandy and kirschwasser, is necessary on mountain excursions: it should be remembered, however, that spirits ought to be resorted to less as a restorative than as a protection against cold and wet, and to mix with water, which ought never to be drunk cold or unmixed during a walk. The best restorative is tea, and as there are many parts of the Alps in which this luxury is hard to find, it is advisable to take a pound or half a pound from England.

JOHN MURRAY, 1745-1793

— 44 —

SHOPPING IN GENEVA

THE shops of Geneva are very tempting to a traveller, being full of such little knick-knacks as he would be glad to carry away in memory of the place; wonderful carvings in wood and ivory, done with exquisite taste and skill; jewellery that seems very cheap, but is doubtless dear enough, if you estimate it by the solid gold that goes into its manufacture; watches, above all things else, for a third or a quarter of the price that one pays in England, – looking just as well, too, and probably performing the whole of a watch's duty as uncriticisably. The Swiss people are frugal and inexpensive in their own habits, I believe, plain and simple, and careless of ornament; but they seem to reckon on other people's spending a great deal of money for gewgaws. We bought some of their wooden trumpery, and likewise a watch for U— ... Next to watches, jewellery, and wood-carving, I should say that cigars were one of the principal articles of commerce in Geneva. Cigar-shops present themselves at every step or two, and at a reasonable rate, there being no duties, I believe, on imported goods. There was no examination of our trunks on arrival, nor any questions asked on that score.

FROM *FRENCH AND ITALIAN NOTEBOOKS* BY NATHANIEL HAWTHORNE, 1804-1864

FLOATING VILLAGES

L ET those who delight in picturesque country, repair to the borders of the Rhine, and follow the road which we took, from Bonn to Coblentz. In some places it is suspended like a cornice, above the waters; in others, it winds behind lofty steeps and broken acclivities, shaded by woods and cloathed with an endless variety of plants and flowers. Several green paths lead amongst this vegetation to the summits of the rocks, which often serve as the foundation of abbeys and castles, whose lofty roofs and spires, rising above the cliffs, impress passengers with ideas of their grandeur, that might probably vanish upon a nearer approach. Not chusing to lose any prejudice in their favour, I kept a respectful distance whenever I left my carriage, and walked on the banks of the river. Just before we came to Andernach, an antiquated town with strange morisco-looking towers, I spied a raft, at least three hundred feet in length, on which ten or twelve cottages were erected, and a great many people employed in sawing wood. The women sat spinning at their doors, whilst their children played among the water-lilies, that bloomed in abundance on the edge of the stream. A smoke, rising from one of these aquatic habitations, partially obscured the mountains beyond, and added not a little to their effect.

FROM *DREAMS, WAKING THOUGHTS, AND INCIDENTS*
BY WILLIAM BECKFORD, 1759-1844

GOTHIC GLORIES

THIS day was passed on board the steamer, going to Mayence. We embarked at ten in the morning. Years had elapsed since I had passed down this river, before steamers were in use – in an ungainly boat, managed in a still more ungainly manner. Memory had painted the Rhine as a scene of enchantment; and the reality came up to what I remembered. The inferior beauty of the banks of the Moselle enhanced still more the prouder and more romantic glories of the Rhine. The promontories stood in bolder relief – the ruined castles and their ramparts were more extensive and more majestic – the antique spires and Gothic abbeys spoke of a princely clergy – and the extent of mouldering walls marked cities belonging to a more powerful population. Each tower-crowned hill – each picturesque ruin – each shadowy ravine and beetling precipice – was passed, and gazed upon with eager curiosity and delight. The very names are the titles of volumes of romance : all the spirits of Old Germany haunt the place. Even the events of modern days have added an interesting tale : – When the German soldiers, led by Blücher, and driving the proud fallen victor before them, beheld the river honoured by them, so late occupied by the enemy they hated, now open and free, the name of "The Rhine!" burst from many thousand voices, accompanied by tears of ecstasy. Some day I should like much to establish myself for a summer on the banks of this river, and explore its recesses. As we glide by, we obtain but a cursory and unsatisfactory survey. One longs to make a familiar friend of such sublime scenery, and refer, in after years, to one's intimate acquaintance with it, as one of the most valued among the treasures of recollection which time may have bestowed.

FROM *RAMBLES IN GERMANY AND ITALY* BY MARY SHELLEY, 1797-1851

A ROYAL SPA

WITH the Germans an excursion to a watering-place in the summer is essential to existence, and the necessity of such a visit is confined to no one class in particular, but pervades all, from Emperors and Princes, down to tradesmen and citizens' wives. The number of bathing places and mineral springs in Germany alone now amounts to several hundred: and every year adds to the list, names, which, though seldom heard in England, are not without their little sets and coteries. The royal and imperial guests repair to them not merely to get rid of the trammels and pomp of sovereignty, though it is universally the case that they move about with no more show than private individuals, but they also seek such occasions for holding private congresses, for forming secret treaties, alliances, &c.; family arrangements and matrimonial connexions are also not unfrequently here concocted. The minister repairs thither to refresh himself from the toils of office, but usually brings his portfolio in his travelling carriage, nor does he altogether even here bid adieu to intrigue and politics. The invalid comes to recruit his strength – the debauchee to wash himself inside and out, and string his nerves for a fresh campaign of dissipation – the shopkeeper and the merchant come to spend their money and gaze on their betters, and the sharper and black-leg, who swarm at all the baths, to enrich themselves at the gaming-tables at the expense of their fellow guests.

FROM *A GUIDE TO THE CONTINENT* BY JOHN MURRAY, 1745-1793

WALKING THROUGH THE
BLACK FOREST

FROM Baden-Baden we made the customary trip into the Black Forest. We were on foot most of the time. One cannot describe those noble woods, nor the feeling with which they inspire him. A feature of the feeling, however, is a deep sense of contentment; another feature of it is a buoyant, boyish gladness; and a third and very conspicuous feature of it is one's sense of the remoteness of the work-day world and his entire emancipation from it and its affairs.

Those woods stretch unbroken over a vast region; and everywhere they are such dense woods, and so still, and so piney and fragrant. The stems of the trees are trim and straight, and in many places all the ground is hidden for miles under a thick cushion of moss of a vivid green colour, with not a decayed or ragged spot in its surface, and not a fallen leaf or twig to mar its immaculate tidiness. A rich cathedral gloom pervades the pillared aisles; so the stray flecks of sunlight that strike a trunk here and a bough yonder are strongly accented, and when they strike the moss they fairly seem to burn. But the weirdest effect, and the most enchanting, is that produced by the diffused light of the low afternoon sun; no single ray is able to pierce its way in, then, but the diffused light takes colour from moss and foliage, and pervades the place like a faint, green-tinted mist, the theatrical fire of fairyland. The suggestion of mystery and the supernatural which haunts the forest at all times is intensified by this unearthly glow.

FROM *A TRAMP ABROAD* BY MARK TWAIN, 1835-1910

VIENNA

PERHAPS of all the great towns I ever was in Vienna is the very pleasantest, particularly at this time of the year. The number of people of fashion who reside here, the ease with which we were introduced, and the many places of public lounging, are beyond those of any town we have seen on the Continent. Bootle introduced us to some friends he had been acquainted with at Petersburg who happened to be here, and we presented our letters to Stratton, the chargé d'affaires. Such an introduction for an Englishman is quite sufficient, as the only question ever asked about you is, "Est-il aimable?" which I presume is the reason why Lord Porchester preferred Dresden, as there can otherwise be no comparison. A few evenings after our arrival we were carried to a great ball at a Madame de Saldaignac's; as she had assembled everything that was gay amongst the *haute noblesse* here, we began in a fair way. The dances in vogue here are the walses, and English country dances, so Heaven be praised we need not, as in France, torture our legs into cotillons, or have a dancing-master to teach us to hold up our heads. The walse, however, we have not yet dared to attempt. I showed Anne one day how it was danced, and if she has forgot Martignier can tell her; but in doing it the other day as part of a country dance I gave my partner such a kick that we were very near both falling together. They dance them so well here that I assure you it was a great subject of lamentation to us that we could not join in them ...

You here meet everybody, for the weather has been uncommonly fine, and people here dare amuse themselves, because it is not thought vulgar. In London it would be certainly thought rather odd, but in a broad, open street like St James's Street I have seen women of fashion, and even princesses with a hundred thousand quarterings, sitting eating ice at a coffee-house door after ten o'clock at night.

FROM *A GRAND TOUR* BY J. B. S. MORRITT, 1772-1843

THE CLASSICAL WORLD

"Italia! oh Italia! thou who hast
The fatal gift of beauty."

LORD BYRON, 1788-1824

ARRIVAL IN ITALY

Milan, April, 1818

BEHOLD us arrived at length at the end of our journey – that is, within a few miles of it – because we design to spend the summer on the shore of the Lake of Como. Our journey was somewhat painful from the cold – and in no other manner interesting until we passed the Alps: of course I except the Alps themselves; but no sooner had we arrived at Italy, than the loveliness of the earth and the serenity of the sky made the greatest difference in my sensations. I depend on these things for life; for in the smoke of cities, and the tumult of human kind, and the chilling fogs and rain of our own country, I can hardly be said to live. With what delight did I hear the woman, who conducted us to see the triumphal arch of Augustus at Susa, speak the clear and complete language of Italy, though half unintelligible to me, after that nasal and abbreviated cacophony of the French! A ruined arch of magnificent proportions in the Greek taste, standing in a kind of road of green lawn, overgrown with violets and primroses, and in the midst of stupendous mountains, and a *blonde* woman, of light and graceful manners, something in the style of Fuseli's Eve, were the first things we met in Italy.

FROM *LETTERS OF P. B. SHELLEY*, 1792-1822

THE BAY OF LERICI

No; the great merit of Spezia, to my eye, is that I engaged a boat there of a lovely October afternoon and had myself rowed across the gulf – it took about an hour and a half – to the little bay of Lerici, which opens out of it. This bay of Lerici is charming; the bosky grey-green hills close it in, and on either side of the entrance, perched on a bold headland, a wonderful old crumbling castle keeps ineffectual guard. The place is classic to all English travellers, for in the middle of the curving shore is the now desolate little villa in which Shelley spent the last months of his short life. He was living at Lerici when he started on that short southern cruise from which he never returned. The house he occupied is strangely shabby and as sad as you may choose to find it. It stands directly upon the beach, with scarred and battered walls and a loggia of several arches opening to a little terrace with a rugged parapet, which, when the wind blows, must be drenched with the salt spray.

The place is very lonely – all overwearied with sun and breeze and brine – very close to nature, as it was Shelley's passion to be. I can fancy a great lyric poet sitting on the terrace of a warm evening and feeling very far from England in the early years of the century. In that place, and with his genius, he would as a matter of course have heard in the voice of nature a sweetness which only the lyric movement could translate. It is a place where an English-speaking pilgrim himself may very honestly think thoughts and feel moved to lyric utterance. But I must content myself with saying in halting prose that I remember few episodes of Italian travel more sympathetic, as they have it here, than that perfect autumn afternoon; the half-hour's station on the little battered terrace of the villa; the climb to the singularly felicitous old castle that hangs above Lerici; the meditative lounge, in the fading light, on the vine-decked platform that looked out toward the sunset and the darkening mountains and, far below, upon the quiet sea, beyond which the pale-faced tragic villa stared up at the brightening moon.

FROM *TRAVELS IN ITALY* BY HENRY JAMES, 1843-1916

VERONA

Pleasant Verona! With its beautiful old palaces, and charming country in the distance, seen from terrace walks, and stately, balustraded galleries. With its Roman gates, still spanning the fair street, and casting, on the sun-light of to-day, the shade of fifteen hundred years ago. With its marble-fitted churches, lofty towers, rich architecture, and quaint old quiet thoroughfares, where shouts of Montagues and Capulets once resounded,

And made Verona's ancient citizens
Cast by their grave beseeming ornaments,
To wield old partisans.

With its fast-rushing river, picturesque old bridge, great castle, waving cypresses, and prospect so delightful and so cheerful! Pleasant Verona!

In the midst of it, in the Piazza di Brá – a spirit of old time among the familiar realities of the passing hour – is the great Roman Amphitheatre. So well preserved and carefully maintained, that every row of seats is there unbroken. Over certain of the arches, the old Roman numerals may yet be seen; and there are corridors, and staircases, and subterranean passages for beasts, and winding ways, above-ground and below, as when the fierce thousands hurried in and out, intent upon the bloody shows of the arena. Nestling in some of the shadows and hollow places of the walls, now, are smiths with their forges, and a few small dealers of one kind or other; and there are green weeds, and leaves, and grass upon the parapet. But little else is greatly changed.

When I had traversed all about it with great interest, and had gone up to the topmost round of seats, and, turning from the lovely panorama closed in by the distant Alps, looked down into the building, it seemed to lie before me like the inside of a prodigious hat of plaited straw, with an enormously broad brim and a shallow crown : the plaits being represented by the four-and-forty rows of seats. The comparison is a homely and fantastic one, in sober remembrance and on paper, but it was irresistibly suggested at the moment, nevertheless.

From *Pictures in Italy* by Charles Dickens, 1812-1870

BRIDGE OF SIGHS

I STOOD in Venice, on the Bridge of Sighs;
A palace and a prison on each hand:
I saw from out the wave her structures rise
As from the stroke of the enchanter's wand:
A thousand years their cloudy wings expand
Around me, and a dying Glory smiles
O'er the far times, when many a subject land
Look'd to the winged Lion's marble piles,
Where Venice sate in state, throned on her hundred isles!

FROM *CHILDE HAROLD'S PILGRIMAGE* BY LORD BYRON, 1788-1824

EVERYDAY VENICE

V ENICE *en fête* is an incomparable thing to see, but to live
with, give me the Venice of every day; for the Venice of
every day is perfect, wanting nothing; and when, in this
world, you get for once anything already perfect, why not be
content with the penny plain, why hanker after the twopence
coloured?

FROM *WANDERINGS* BY ARTHUR SYMONS, 1865-1945

THE GRAND CANAL

THE *ricordi* of Venice that we prefer are gathering best where the gondola glides – best of all on the noble waterway that begins in its glory at the Salute and ends in its abasement at the railway station. It is, however, the Piazzetta that introduces us most directly to the great picture by which the Grand Canal works its first spell, and to which a thousand artists, not always with a talent apiece, have paid their tribute. We pass into the Piazzetta to look down the great throat, as it were, of Venice, and the vision must console us for turning our back on St Mark's ...

The classic Salute waits like some great lady on the threshold of her salon. She is more ample and serene, more seated at her door, than all the copyists have told us, with her domes and scrolls, her scolloped buttresses and statues forming a pompous crown, and her wide steps disposed on the ground like the train of a robe. This fine air of the woman of the world is carried out by the well-bred assurance with which she looks in the direction of her old-fashioned Byzantine neighbor; and the juxtaposition of two churches so distinguished and so different, each splendid in its sort, is a sufficient mark of the scale and range of Venice.

FROM *TRAVELS IN ITALY* BY HENRY JAMES, 1843-1916

A TOCCATA OF GALUPPI'S

OH Galuppi, Baldassaro, this is very sad
   to find!
I can hardly misconceive you; it would
   prove me deaf and blind:
But although I take your meaning, 'tis
   with such a heavy mind!

Here you come with your old music, and
   here's all the good it brings.
What, they lived once thus at Venice where
   the merchants were the kings,
Where Saint Mark's is, where the Doges
   used to wed the sea with rings?

Did young people take their pleasure when
   the sea was warm in May?
Balls and masks begun at midnight, burning
   ever to mid-day,
When they made up fresh adventures for
   the morrow, do you say?

Was a lady such a lady, cheeks so round
   and lips so red, –
On her neck the small face buoyant, like
   a bell-flower on its bed,
O'er the breast's superb abundance where
   a man might base his head?

" As for Venice and her people, merely born
   to bloom and drop,
" Here on earth they bore their fruitage,
   mirth and folly were the crop:
" What of soul was left, I wonder, when the
   kissing had to stop?

ROBERT BROWNING, 1812–1889

A ROOM WITH A VIEW

IT was pleasant to wake up in Florence, to open the eyes upon a bright bare room, with a floor of red tiles which look clean though they are not; with a painted ceiling whereon pink griffins and blue amorini sport in a forest of yellow violins and bassoons. It was pleasant, too, to fling wide the windows, pinching the fingers in unfamiliar fastenings, to lean out into sunshine with beautiful hills and trees and marble churches opposite, and, close below, the Arno, gurgling against the embankment of the road.

Over the river men were at work with spades and sieves on the sandy foreshore, and on the river was a boat, also diligently employed for some mysterious end. An electric tram came rushing underneath the window. No one was inside it, except one tourist; but its platforms were overflowing with Italians, who preferred to stand. Children tried to hang on behind, and the conductor, with no malice, spat in their faces to make them let go. Then soldiers appeared – good-looking, undersized men – wearing each a knapsack covered with mangy fur, and a greatcoat which had been cut for some larger soldier. Beside them walked officers, looking foolish and fierce, and before them went little boys, turning somersaults in time with the band. The tram-car became entangled in their ranks, and moved on painfully, like a caterpillar in a swarm of ants. One of the little boys fell down, and some white bullocks came out of an archway. Indeed, if it had not been for the good advice of an old man who was selling buttonhooks, the road might never have got clear.

Over such trivialities as these many a valuable hour may slip away, and the traveller who has gone to Italy to study the tactile values of Giotto, or the corruption of the Papacy, may return remembering nothing but the blue sky and the men and women who live under it.

FROM *A ROOM WITH A VIEW* BY E. M. FORSTER. 1879-1970

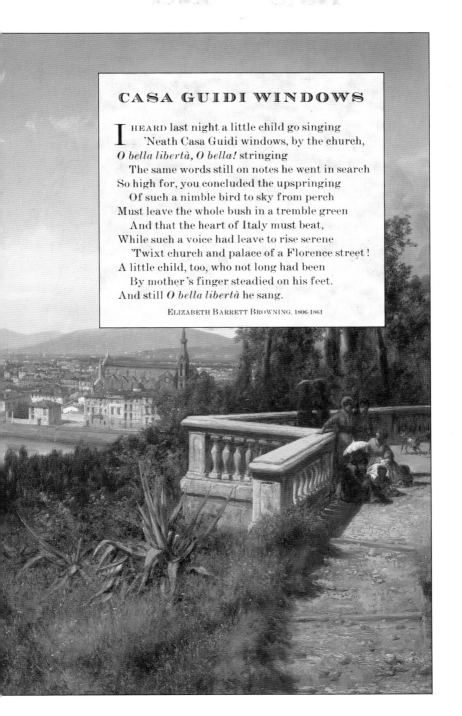

CASA GUIDI WINDOWS

I HEARD last night a little child go singing
   'Neath Casa Guidi windows, by the church,
O bella libertà, O bella! stringing
   The same words still on notes he went in search
So high for, you concluded the upspringing
   Of such a nimble bird to sky from perch
Must leave the whole bush in a tremble green
   And that the heart of Italy must beat,
While such a voice had leave to rise serene
   'Twixt church and palace of a Florence street!
A little child, too, who not long had been
   By mother's finger steadied on his feet.
And still *O bella libertà* he sang.

ELIZABETH BARRETT BROWNING, 1806-1861

HEALTH MATTERS

IN the height of summer they should avoid excessive exposure to the sun and they may wear coloured spectacles with advantage. In winter, as there is a great difference between the sun and the shade temperatures, an overcoat, though perhaps unnecessary out-of-doors, will often be needed on entering cold churches and galleries; on warmer days it is also advisable to drive to such places and walk back, in order to get warm again. Sunless rooms facing N. should be avoided in winter, and a sufficiency of bed-clothes should be stipulated for. Moderation in diet should be observed. Cheese, macaroni, shell-fish, and iced drinks should be sparingly partaken of. In hot weather especially, sea-fish, when not quite fresh, salads, unpeeled fruit, and, above all, oysters are often harmful. Although the larger cities have a good water supply, the traveller should be on his guard against bad drinking-water (especially in the Apennines). The safest drink is the red wine of the country or mineral water. Lastly, a word of warning against hurry, as over-exertion, particularly in summer, often brings on the illnesses from which travellers in Italy suffer. At the first symptom of indisposition all excursions should be given up, and, if need be, a physician consulted.

FROM *ITALY: A HANDBOOK FOR TRAVELLERS* BY KARL BAEDEKER, 1801-1859

" TUT, tut! Miss Lucy! I hope we shall soon emancipate you
from Baedeker. He does but touch the surface of things.
As to the true Italy – he does not even dream of it. The true
Italy is only to be found by patient observation."

FROM *A ROOM WITH A VIEW* BY E. M. FORSTER, 1879-1970

THE BOBOLI GARDENS

JUNE 21st. – Yesterday, after dinner, we went with the two eldest children to the Boboli Gardens ... We entered by a gate nearer to our house than that by the Pitti Palace, and found ourselves almost immediately among embowered walks of box and shrubbery, and little wildernesses of trees, with here and there a seat under an arbour, and a marble statue, grey with ancient weather-stains. The site of the garden is a very uneven surface, and the paths go upward and downward, and ascend, at their ultimate point, to a base of what appears to be a fortress, commanding the city. A good many of the Florentines were rambling about the gardens, like ourselves; little parties of schoolboys, fathers and mothers, with their youthful progeny ; young men in couples, looking closely into every female face; lovers, with a maid or two attendant on the young lady. All appeared to enjoy themselves, especially the children, dancing on the esplanades, or rolling down the slopes of the hills; and the loving pairs, whom it was rather embarrassing to come upon unexpectedly, sitting together on the stone seat of an arbour, with clasped hands; a passionate solemnity in the young man's face, and a downcast pleasure in the lady's. Policemen, in cocked hats and epaulettes, cross-belts, and swords, were scattered about the grounds, but interfered with nobody, though they seemed to keep an eye on all. A sentinel stood in the hot sunshine, looking down over the garden from the ramparts of the fortress.

FROM *FRENCH AND ITALIAN NOTEBOOKS* BY NATHANIEL HAWTHORNE, 1804-1864

SUN IN SIENA

To Ralph the Sienese air was not only breathable but intoxicating. The sun, treading the earth like a vintager, drew from it heady fragrances, crushed out of it new colours. All the values of the temperate landscape were reversed : the noon high-lights were white, but the shadows had unimagined colour. On the blackness of cork and ilex and cypress lay the green and purple lustres, the coppery iridescences, of old bronze ; and night after night the skies were wine-blue and bubbling with stars. Ralph said to himself that no one who had not seen Italy thus prostrate beneath the sun knew what secret treasures she could yield.

FROM *THE CUSTOM OF THE COUNTRY* BY EDITH WHARTON, 1862-1937

FIREWORKS

THE next night – Easter Monday – there was a great display of fireworks from the Castle of St Angelo. We hired a room in an opposite house, and made our way to our places in good time, through a dense mob of people choking up the square in front, and all the avenues leading to it; and so loading the bridge by which the castle is approached, that it seemed ready to sink into the rapid Tiber below. There are statues on this bridge (execrable works), and, among them, great vessels full of burning tow were placed: glaring strangely on the faces of the crowd, and not less strangely on the stone counterfeits above them.

The show began with a tremendous discharge of cannon; and then, for twenty minutes, or half an hour, the whole castle was one incessant sheet of fire, and labyrinth of blazing wheels of every colour, size, and speed: while rockets streamed into the sky, not by ones or twos, or scores, but hundreds at a time. The concluding burst – the Girandola – was like the blowing up into the air of the whole massive castle, without smoke or dust.

FROM *PICTURES IN ITALY* BY CHARLES DICKENS, 1812-1870

FIRST IMPRESSIONS
OF ROME

I MAY not attempt to report in its fulness our young woman's response to the deep appeal of Rome, to analyse her feelings as she trod the pavement of the Forum or to number her pulsations as she crossed the threshold of Saint Peter's. It is enough to say that her impression was such as might have been expected of a person of her freshness and her eagerness. She had always been fond of history, and here was history in the stones of the street and the atoms of the sunshine. She had an imagination that kindled at the mention of great deeds, and wherever she turned some great deed had been acted. These things strongly moved her, but moved her all inwardly. It seemed to her companions that she talked less than usual, and Ralph Touchett, when he appeared to be looking listlessly and awkwardly over her head, was really dropping on her an intensity of observation. By her own measure she was very happy; she would even have been willing to take these hours for the happiest she was ever to know. The sense of the terrible human past was heavy to her, but that of something altogether contemporary would suddenly give it wings that it could wave in the blue.

FROM *THE PORTRAIT OF A LADY* BY HENRY JAMES. 1843-1916

THE HILLS OF ROME

WHEN you gain the summit of yonder hill, you will discover Rome, said one of the postillions: up we dragged; no city appeared. From the next, cried out a second; and so on, from height to height, did they amuse my expectations. I thought Rome fled before us, such was my impatience; till, at last, we perceived a cluster of hills, with green pastures on their summits, inclosed by thickets, and shaded by flourishing ilex. Here and there, a white house, built in the antient style, with open porticos, that received a faint gleam of the evening sun, just emerged from the clouds and tinting the meads below. Now, domes and towers began to discover themselves in the valley, and St Peter's to rise above the magnificent roofs of the Vatican. Every step we advanced, the scene extended; till, winding suddenly round the hill, all Rome opened to our view. A spring flowed opportunely into a marble cistern close by the way; two cypresses and a pine waved over it. I leaped out, poured water upon my hands, and then, lifting them up to the sylvan Genii of the place, implored their protection. I wished to run wild in the fresh fields and copses above the Vatican, there to have remained, till fauns might peep out of their conceal-ments, and satyrs begin to touch their flutes in the twilight; for the place looks still so wonderous classical, that I can never persuade myself, either Constantine, Attila, or the Popes themselves, have chased them all away. I think I should have found some out, who would have fed me with milk and chestnuts, have sung me a Latin ditty, and mourned the woeful changes which have taken place, since their sacred groves were felled, and Faunus ceased to be oracular. Who can tell but they would have given me some mystic skin to sleep on, that I might have looked into futurity? Shall I ever forget the sensations I experienced, upon slowly descending the hills, and crossing the bridge over the Tyber, when I entered an avenue between terraces and ornamented gates of villas, which leads to the Porto del Popolo? and beheld the square, the domes, the obelisk; the long perspective of streets and palaces opening beyond, all glowing with the vivid red of sun-set? You can imagine how I enjoyed my beloved tint, my favourite hour, surrounded by such objects.

FROM *DREAMS, WAKING THOUGHTS, AND INCIDENTS* BY WILLIAM BECKFORD 1759-1844

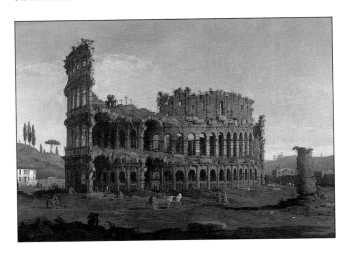

GROTTO AZZURRO, CAPRI

TO-DAY we visited Capri.... In two hours we reached the island, and ran into the little bay in which the town of Capri is situated. We then transferred ourselves to two small boats, for the purpose of visiting the Grotto Azzurro. We were rowed under the high, dark, bare, perpendicular cliffs, and with anxious curiosity I looked for the opening to the grotto. The mountains grew higher, the precipices more abrupt and black, as we rowed slowly in the deep calm water beneath their shadow. At length we came to a small opening; it was necessary to sit at the bottom of the boat, as it shot through the narrow, low, covered entrance; within, the strangest sight is revealed : we entered a large cavern, formed by the sea; the hue resembles that which I mentioned as belonging to the caves of the Sorrentine coast; only here it is brighter — a turquoise, milky, pellucid, living azure. The white roof and walls of the cave reflect the tints, and the shimmering motion of the waves being also mirrored on the rock, the effect is more fairy-like and strange than can be conceived. This cave was discovered by two Englishmen, who went to swim under the cliffs, and penetrated by chance its narrow opening. It deserves the renown it has gained. I cannot explain from what effect of the laws of light this singular and beautiful hue proceeds. Partly it is the natural azure of the waves of this bright sea, which, entering, reflects the snow-white cavern, and is turned as it were into transparent milk ; another cause may be, that the walls of the cavern do not reach deeper than the surface of the water ; they just touch it – and the sea flows beneath. The water is icy cold, and the adventure would be perilous ; but a good swimmer might be excited to dive beneath the paving water, strike out under the cave, and seek for wonders beyond.

FROM *RAMBLES IN GERMANY AND ITALY* BY MARY SHELLEY, 1797-1851

MOUNT VESUVIUS

Y<small>OU</small> may be surprised that I have said so little about Vesuvius. Notwithstanding my silence, we have not passed a day, scarcely an hour, unless at night, – and many hours of the latter even are an exception, – without having this beautiful mountain under our eyes. I say beautiful, for, including its base, loaded with towns, palaces, ruins, villages, and villas, – its sides seamed with ravines, and occasionally smiling with verdure, or dark with forests, – and its cone of cinders, – it forms altogether an object of great attraction. By day, there is usually a light cloud of smoke rising from the water, and hovering above it; and by night, occasional flashes illumine the sky and the mouth of the mountain in a way that the fire of a forge brightens and sinks in the darkness. I do not think we have seen any positive flame; but of late we have had brighter gleamings from beneath than are usual.

The heat of the weather had hitherto prevented an attempt

to ascend; but W—— and myself determined, not long since, that it was time to make the excursion. To this end we crossed the bay to Naples, and passed the night in town, having also an early start in view. Accordingly we drove to Portici, where we breakfasted. We then mounted our horses, under the protection of a guide of reputation, and proceeded. The ascent for four or five miles is gradual; the road, an indifferent one at the best, and nearly impracticable for wheels, leads at first through vineyards, then among copses, and often along water-courses, or across beds of ancient lava. The summit of the mountain is the cone of which I have spoken. Its form is regular, though the edges are broken, some portions being much higher than others, though the side nearest Naples and the bay, just now, is tolerably even. I believe the perpendicular height of the lowest part of this cone is about eight hundred feet; though it varies materially at different times. From its base, a ridge runs in a westerly direction for the distance of a mile, when it falls away rapidly towards the plain.

FROM *EXCURSIONS IN ITALY* BY JAMES FENIMORE COOPER, 1789-1851

THE ISLES OF GREECE

THE isles of Greece, the isles of Greece!
　　Where burning Sappho loved and sung,
Where grew the arts of war and peace,
　　Where Delos rose, and Phoebus sprung!
Eternal summer gilds them yet,
But all, except their sun, is set.

The Scian and the Teian muse,
　　The hero's harp, the lover's lute,
Have found the fame your shores refuse :
　　Their place of birth alone is mute
To sounds which echo further west
Than your sires' " Island of the Blest ".

The mountains look on Marathon –
　　And Marathon looks on the sea ;
And musing there an hour alone,
　　I dream'd that Greece might still be free ;
For standing on the Persians' grave,
I could not deem myself a slave.

LORD BYRON. 1788-1824

PEIRAEUS

IT was our fortune to come into Greece by night, with a splendid moon shining upon the summer sea. The varied outlines of Sunium, on the one side, and Ægina on the other, were very clear, but in the deep shadows there was mystery enough to feed the burning impatience to see it all in the light of common day; and though we had passed Ægina, and had come over against the rocky Salamis, as yet there was no sign of Peiræus. Then came the light on Psyttalea, and they told us that the harbour was right opposite. Yet we came nearer and nearer, and no harbour could be seen. The barren rocks of the coast seemed to form one unbroken line, and nowhere was there a sign of indentation or of break in the land. But, suddenly, as we turned from gazing on Psyttalea, where the flower of the Persian nobles had once stood in despair, looking upon their fate gathering about them, the vessel had turned eastward, and discovered to us the crowded lights and thronging ships of the famous harbour. Small it looked, very small, but evidently deep to the water's edge, for great ships seemed touching the shore; and so narrow is the mouth, that we almost wondered how they had made their entrance in safety. But we saw it some weeks later, with nine men-of-war towering above all its merchant shipping and its steamers, and among them crowds of ferry-boats skimming about in the breeze with their wing-like sails. Then we found out that, like the rest of Greece, the Peiræus was far larger than it looked.

FROM *RAMBLES AND STUDIES IN GREECE* BY J. P. MAHAFFY, 1839-1919

THE GILDED LAKE

Soon a new world charmed the eye, and on arriving at the edge of the western face of this high ridge, the beautiful plain and lake of Akhridha burst, as it were, into existence; gilded in the setting sun, and slumbering below hills, forest, and snow, piled up and mingled with cloud midway in heaven. It is scarcely possible to dream of finer scenes than these, their beauty perhaps enhanced by grand storm effects, which gave them more than ordinary magic of colour and variety of interest. Bright, broad, and long lay the great sheet of water – the first of Grecian lakes – and on its edge the fortress and town of Akhridha (in form singularly resembling the castle rock of Nice, in the Sardinian States), commanding the cultivated plain which stretches from the mountains to the shores of the lake. Such sublime scenery obliterated from the memory all annoyances of travel, and astonished and delighted at every step, I already repented of my repentance that I had undertaken this journey.

FROM *JOURNALS OF A LANDSCAPE PAINTER IN GREECE AND ALBANIA*
BY EDWARD LEAR, 1812-1888

A GREEK WELCOME

IN their intercourse with strangers the Greeks are friendly,
civil, and, as a rule, not officious or importunate, though
the male inhabitants of a village, old and young, may
sometimes show their curiosity by clustering round the
traveller. Offers of service, such as are common in Italy, are
rare. The tourist therefore pursues his way without molesta-
tion, though, when his time is limited, he may miss the sharp
little Italian ragazzi, who seem to divine the stranger's
intentions by instinct and conduct him to the wished for spots
for a fee of a few soldi. The inordinate idea of the importance
of travellers that prevails in S. Italy is also found in Greece;
and the lower classes cherish a firm conviction that every
foreigner (λορδος, "lord") is enormously rich.

KARL BAEDEKER, 1801-1859

ESSENTIAL PACKING

THE traveller is strongly recommended to take with him a supply of curry-powder, a bottle of Worcestershire sauce, and a few pots of marmalade. These three items will often make all the difference between an eatable and an uneatable meal. Butter is unknown (except for cooking purposes) in the provinces of Greece, and even in Athens the substance served under that name at table much more nearly resembles an inferior kind of Devonshire cream.

FROM *MURRAY'S HANDBOOK FOR TRAVELLERS IN GREECE* BY JOHN MURRAY, 1745-1793

NEGLECTED BEAUTY

WE soon had a full view of Athens, the approach to which throws your mind quite back to ancient times. The first object that strikes you on approaching the town from every side is the citadel. Its present walls, built by the Venetians on the ancient foundations, enclose the top of a high insulated rock, containing eight or ten acres. Over these domineer the remains of the temple of Minerva, of which the front is entire and most of the other pillars standing, from the side by which we came; the smaller pillars of another little temple (of Erechtheus) are also seen in the citadel. The road, about a mile from Athens, passes a small hill, where was the famous Academy; beyond these we could see the whole town, which is still considerable, and the remains and monuments round it. Its situation, independent of beauty, is the driest and best chosen I can conceive, sloping every way from the rocks of the citadel and covering the sides of some other low hills near, in a clear climate and a gravelly soil. The object which, next to the citadel, embellishes it most is the little [so-called] temple of Theseus on a low, green hill at the end of the town. It is absolutely entire, and is at present a modern Greek church. The only changes it has undergone is in roofing the inside, which was in the ancient temple, I believe, open, and the unroofing of the portico between the pillars and the body of the temple, where the people assisted at the sacrifices.

These make no alteration in its form; it is oblong, built entirely of marble. It is, I believe, about sixty feet in length and half that in width, and at the end of the entrance are two columns supporting a beautiful frieze in basso-rilievo. The sculptures representing the combats of Theseus with the Amazons, and different circumstances of his life, are, I believe, as well as those in the citadel, the work of Phidias.

The heads of all are mutilated, and it must have taken some pains to destroy them so much. Indeed, I hear they were destroyed prior to the Turks, in the barbarous ages of Christianity, and by order of the Greek Emperors, who, adopting the zeal of the iconoclasts, broke them as idolatrous; and, indeed, the Turks, though they repair nothing, generally don't give themselves much trouble to destroy things placed so high as these are, which seems rather to have required the animation of bigotry, as well as the blindness of barbarism. Would you believe, however, that the Turks have lately been breaking up part of the white marble flags that surround the temple, merely to burn into lime, because it is nearer at hand than most other limestone?

FROM *A GRAND TOUR* BY J. B. S. MORRITT. 1772-1843

THE ACROPOLIS AT DAWN

I ROSE at the break of dawn to see whether the window would afford any prospect to serve as a requital for angry sleeplessness. And there, right opposite, stood the rock which of all rocks in the world's history has done most for literature and art – the rock which poets, and orators, and architects, and historians have ever glorified, and cannot stay their praise – which is ever new and ever old, ever fresh in its decay, ever perfect in its ruin, ever living in its death – the Acropolis of Athens.

When I saw my dream and longing of many years fulfilled, the first rays of the rising sun had just touched the heights, while the town below was still hid in gloom. Rock, and rampart, and ruined fanes – all were coloured in uniform tints; the lights were of a deep rich orange, and the shadows of dark crimson, with the deeper lines of purple. There was no variety in colour between what nature and what man had set there. No whiteness shone from the marble, no smoothness showed upon the hewn and polished blocks; but the whole mass of orange and vast, great scarlet poppies stained the ground in patches as it were with slaughter, and hawks and ravens were still circling about overhead, as their ancestors did in the days of blood; attached, I suppose, by hereditary instinct to this fatal place, "for where the carcase is, there shall the eagles be gathered together."

FROM *RAMBLES AND STUDIES IN GREECE* BY J. P. MAHAFFY, 1839-1919

A GREEK SOJOURN

Patras, July 30, 1810

THE heat is at present intense. In England, if it reaches 98° you are all on fire: the other day, in travelling between Athens and Megara, the thermometer was at 125°!!! Yet I feel no inconvenience; of course I am much bronzed, but I live temperately, and never enjoyed better health. . . .

I have a tolerable suite, a Tartar, two Albanians, an interpreter, besides Fletcher; but in this country these are easily maintained. Adair received me wonderfully well, and indeed I have no complaints against any one. Hospitality here is necessary, for inns are not. I have lived in the houses of Greeks, Turks, Italians, and English – to-day in a palace, to-morrow in a cow-house; this day with a Pacha, the next with a shepherd. I shall continue to write briefly, but frequently, and am glad to hear from you; but you fill your letters with things from the papers, as if English papers were not found all over the world. I have at this moment a dozen before me. Pray take care of my books, and believe me, my dear mother,

Yours very faithfully,

BYRON.

LORD BYRON, LETTER TO HIS MOTHER, 1788-1824

A VISIT TO THE PASHA

WE went in the evening, and found an immense and mean-looking range of buildings round a large court, which was the Pasha's palace. The court was lighted very well by pans of blazing tar set up on poles. We found an amazing number of Turks of all ranks walking in a dirty gallery behind the house, open, with sheds like a booth, to the court. We went to the dragoman's office attended by ours, for his only speaks Greek and Turkish. While we were here a Turkish buffoon came in to make us laugh, as he did the Pasha, and danced, imitating lameness, etc., with a thousand grimacings and face-makings of this same style. The dragoman gives him, and almost all the lower people of the house, money every week, and the other greater officers do the same; this is the way a Pasha's servants are paid. After coffee and pipes we went to the Kiaya, or second under the Pasha. He received us in a large room sofa'd round with a red carpet of cloth. On entering his, or indeed any room, you take off your slippers, and walk in short yellow-leather socks, which are a part of a Turkish dress. We here found our friend the Aga we had been with before, sat down, and drank our coffee, which is brought always. Our dragomans and all the people that attend on the Kiaya stood while we stayed. We then returned to the dragoman's again to wait till the Pasha was ready. It is sometimes a mark of his dignity to make you wait a long time.

We at last were introduced, and took our seats on the low sofa, everybody besides standing in the room. Two boys brought us round a very fine covered vase of china and a spoon; we concluded the sweetmeats must be excellent, but unfortunately it was nothing but a little pounded sugar. The sweetmeats, we supposed, had been changed by the boys that have the serving them, and taken for themselves.

FROM *A GRAND TOUR* BY J. B. S. MORRITT, 1772-1843

HOME THOUGHTS
FROM ABROAD

O TO be in England
  Now that April's there,
And whoever wakes in England
Sees, some morning, unaware,
That the lowest boughs and the brushwood sheaf
Round the elm-tree bole are in tiny leaf,
While the chaffinch sings on the orchard bough
In England – now!

ROBERT BROWNING, 1812-1889

NEW YORK HARBOUR

WE crossed to England, and then made the homeward passage in the Cunarder "Gallia", a very fine ship. I was glad to get home – immeasurably glad; so glad, in fact, that it did not seem possible that anything could ever get me out of the country again. I had not enjoyed a pleasure abroad which seemed to me to compare with the pleasure I felt in seeing New York harbour again. Europe has many advantages which we have not, but they do not compensate for a good many still more valuable ones which exist nowhere but in our own country. Then we are such a homeless lot when we are over there! So are Europeans themselves, for that matter. They live in dark and chilly vast tombs, costly enough, maybe, but without conveniences. To be condemned to live as the average European family lives would make life a pretty heavy burden to the average American family.

FROM *A TRAMP ABROAD* BY MARK TWAIN, 1835-1910

ACKNOWLEDGEMENTS

Birmingham City Museum & Art Gallery :
p83 *Firework Display at the Castel St Angelo* : Joseph Wright of Derby.

Bridgeman Art Library :
p3 *The Campanile and the Doge's Palace with St Mark's in the Background* :
James R W S Holland/Roy Miles Fine Paintings, London ; p4 *Goodbye on the
Mersey* : James Jacques Tissot/Forbes Magazine Collection, NY ; p5 *The Ball on
Shipboard* : James Jacques Tissot/Tate Gallery ; p6-7 *Travelling Companions* :
Augustus Egg/Birmingham City Art Gallery ; p11 *The Bookworm* : Henry
Stacy Marks/Chris Beetles Ltd, London ; p12-13 *Outside the Théatre du
Vaudeville, Paris* : Jean Beraud/Tate Gallery ; p15 *Waiting for the Boat* : James
Jacques Tissot/Owen Edgar Gallery, London ; p18-19 *In the Luxembourg
Gardens, Paris* : Albert Edelfelt/Art Museum of the Atheneum, Helsinki ; p23
After Paris, Queen Victoria after the Opera : Edmund Thomas/Forbes Magazine
Collection, NY ; p24 *Dance at Bougival* : Pierre Auguste Renoir/Museum of
Fine Arts, Boston ; p29 *Rouen Cathedral* : Lewis John Wood/Gavin Graham
Gallery, London ; p33 *The Laundress* : Edouard Frere/Haworth Art Gallery,
Accrington ; p34 *Entrance to the Port of Marseilles* : William Callow/Towneley
Hall Art Gallery & Museum ; p35 *Collioure* : J D Innes/Bradford City Art
Gallery & Museums ; p38 *The Wanderer* : Casper David Friedrich/Kunsthalle,
Hamburg ; p39 *An Alpine Lake* : Karl Millner/Christie's, London ; p42 *Spring
Mountain Flowers* : Kate Goodwin/Chris Beetles Ltd, London ; p46-47 *A Village
Fête in the Rhine Valley* : Jan, the elder Griffier/Johnny Van Haeften Gallery ;
p48 *The Castle of Katz on the Rhine* : William Callow/Bonham's, London ; p51
The Bath : Alfred George Stevens/Musée D'Orsay, Paris ; p56-57 *The Terrace,
Capri* : Karl Maria Schuster/Waterhouse & Dodd, London ; p58-59 *Lake Como* :
Gustave Mascart/Cider House Galleries Ltd, London ; p61 *Confidences on the
Beach* : Vincente Palmaroli/Prado, Madrid ; p62 *Piazza dei Signori, Verona with
the Market Place* : James R W S Holland/Royal Holloway and Bedford New
College, London ; p64 *Bridge of Sighs* : William Etty/City of York Art Gallery ;
p65 *Venice* : Gaston Hippolyte Boucaart/Gavin Graham Gallery, London ; p67
By the Canal, Venice : Marcus Stone/Roy Miles Fine Paintings, London ; p68-69
The Campanile and the Doge's Palace with St Mark's in the Background : James
R W S Holland/Roy Miles Fine Paintings, London ; p70 *The Basilica of San
Marco, Venice* : Fernand Legont-Gerard/Waterhouse & Dodd, London ; p71
Venice, Flood Tide : Arthur Joseph Meadows/David Messum Fine Paintings,
London ; p73 *A Masked Ball in a Theatre* : Alois Schonn/Christie's, London ; p75
At the Window : Hans Heyerdahl/Nasjonalgalleriet, Oslo ; p76-77 *Florence* :
Andreas Marko/Christie's, London ; p79 *Two Women Admiring the Town of
Florence* : Edouard Menta/Christie's, London ; p81 *By the Pitti Palace,
Florence* : Antonietta Brandeis/Waterhouse & Dodd, London ; p82 *View of a
Roman Villa* : Jean Achille Benouville/Musée D'Orsay, Paris ; p84-85 *The
Forum, Rome* : Gustav Palm/Bonham's, London ; p87 *Colosseum and the Arch of
Constantine, Rome* : Giovanni Antonio Canaletto/Private Collection ; p88-89
Amalfi : Carl Frederick Aagaard/Christie's, London ; p93 *On Shipboard* :
Theodore Jacques Ralli/Christie's, London ; p94-95 *Thermopylae* : Edward
Lear/City of Bristol Museums & Art Galleries ; p96 *A Contented Mind's a
Continual Feast* : Nicol Erskine/Harrogate Museums & Art Galleries ; p97 *Le
Recontre or Bonjour M. Courbet* (detail) : Gustave Courbet/Musée Fabre
Montpellier ; p100 *The Acropolis* : Carl Haag/City of Bristol Museums & Art

Galleries ; p101 *Lord Byron Dressed in Greek Apparel* : Thomas Phillips/ Private Collection ; p103 *Lord Byron* : David Allan/Roy Miles Fine Paintings, London ; p104-105 *One of the People, an Incident in the Life of The Right Honourable William Ewart Gladstone* : Christie's, London ; p109 *Luggage Boat on Lake Geneva* : Lamorna-Birch/Courtesy of the Trustees of the V&A, London ; p110 *Count Robert of Montesquiou* : Giovanni Boldini/Musée D'Orsay, Paris.

Fine Art Photographic Archive :
p1 *Where Next?* : Edward Frederick Brewtnall ; p9 *Palm Court* : Henri Gerbault ; p16 *Figures on a Street in a French Coastal Town* : Luigi Loir ; p20 *Rendezvous in the Bois de Boulogne* : Auguste De Molins ; p21 *The Morning Ride in the Bois de Boulogne* : Edmond Georges Grandjean ; p25 *The Salon Lunch* : Jean André Rixens ; p26-27 *Le Chateau de Chenonceau* : Pierre Justin Ouverie ; p28 *The Egg Stall* : Fritz Schnitzler ; p36-37 *A View of Schliersee* : W Scheachzer ; p40 *Le Chateau de Chillon* : Gustave Courbet ; p43 *An Alpine Village* : Emil Rau ; p44 *Ribbons and Laces* : Edward C Clifford ; p45 *View of the Corner Glacier and Zermatt Valley* : François Zavier Roffiaen ; p53 *Figures by a Woodland Stream* : Gustave Dore ; p54-55 *An Elegant Soirée* : Albert Chevalier Tayler ; p66 *La Venezia* : Cesare Laurenti ; p78 *Solitude* : Louis Emile Pinel de Grandchamp ; p90-91 *View of the Bay of Naples and Vesuvius* : Hermann David Salomon Corrodi ; p92 *Noonday Rest* : John William Godward ; p99 *Athens, The Temple of Minerva* : Lancelot Theodore Turpin de Crisse.

Fine Arts Society :
p86 *The Hills of Rome* : Johann Jakob Frey.

Private Collection, Courtesy of David Messum Fine Paintings, London :
p31 *The Honeymoon* : Sir John Lavery.

Museum of the City of New York :
p107 *Unveiling of the Statue of Liberty* : Edward Moran.

Worcester Art Museum, USA :
p2 *Gentleman in a Railway Carriage* : James Jacques Tissot.

Cover : *On Board HMS Calcutta* : James Jacques Tissot/Tate Gallery.

PENHALIGON'S
EAU DE COLOGNE

IN the latter half of the seventeenth century, Eau de Cologne was created by an Italian, Jean-Paul Feminis. When he settled in Cologne, he passed on the formula to his nephew, Jean Maria Farina, who produced it under the name of Eau de Cologne.

French soldiers returning from the Seven Years' War brought Eau de Cologne to France. There it was favoured by Napoleon, who used it to freshen up throughout his campaigns, and he is reputed to have used sixty bottles each month.

Penhaligon's Eau de Cologne is a classic. A bouquet of citrus oils blended with herbaceous notes, it is refreshing and delightful but, by nature, of short duration.

S.P.

First published in Great Britain in 1991 by
PAVILION BOOKS LIMITED
196 Shaftesbury Avenue
London WC2H 8JL

Selection and Introduction copyright © Sheila Pickles 1991
Pages 74 & 79 : From A ROOM WITH A VIEW by E M Forster,
reproduced by permission of Edward Arnold Publishers

Designed by Bernard Higton
Picture research by Lynda Marshall

A CIP catalogue record for this book is available
from the British Library

ISBN 1-85145-572-8

Printed and bound in Hong Kong

10 9 8 7 6 5 4 3 2 1

For more information about Penhaligon's perfumes,
please telephone London (071) 836 2150 or write to :
PENHALIGON'S
41 Wellington Street
Covent Garden
London WC2

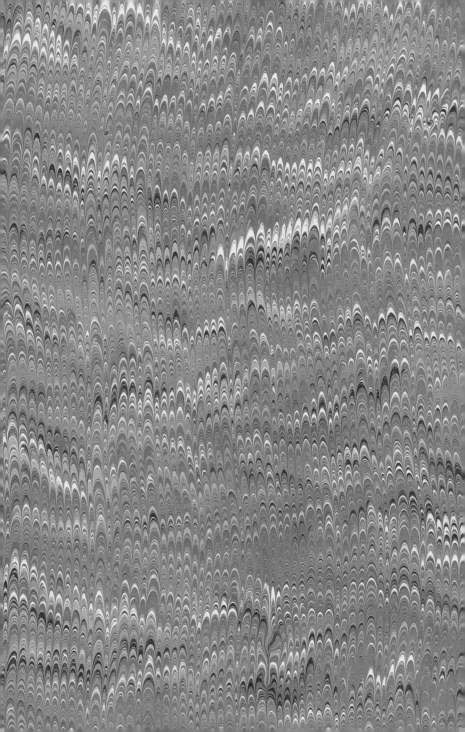